FIRST AMERICANS

The Powhatan

DAVID C. KING

Marshall Cavendish
Benchmark
New York

ACKNOWLEDGMENTS

Series consultant: Raymond Bial

Marshall Cavendish Benchmark
99 White Plains Road
Tarrytown, New York 10591-9001
www.marshallcavendish.us

Text copyright © 2008 by Marshall Cavendish Corp.
Map and illustrations copyright © 2008 by Marshall Cavendish Corp.
Map and illustration by Rodica Prato
Craft illustrations by Chris Santoro

Library of Congress Cataloging-in-Publication Data
King, David C.
The Powhatan / by David C. King.
p. cm. — (First Americans)
Summary: "Provides comprehensive information on the background, lifestyle,
beliefs, and present-day lives of the Powhatan people"—Provided by publisher.
Includes bibliographical references and index.
ISBN-13: 978-0-7614-2681-3
1. Powhatan Indians—Juvenile literature. I. Title. II. Series.
E99.P85K56 2007
975.5004'97347—dc22
2006034115

On the cover: A young girl practices traditional dance steps at a Native American festival in Virginia.
Title page: This is a detail of a "jingle dress," worn at an Upper Mattaponi tribe powwow.

Photo Research by Connie Gardner
Cover photo by Stan Honda/AFP/Getty Images
The photographs in this book are used by permission and through the courtesy of: Getty Images: AFP, 1,39; Hulton Archive, 4; National Geographic, 19(B). Granger Collection: 8, 13, 20, 33. Nativestock.com: Marilyn "Angel" Wynn, 18, 19 (T), 23, 26, 28, 35, 36. North Wind Picture Archive: 10, 14. Corbis: David Muench, 16.

Editor: Deborah Grahame
Publisher: Michelle Bisson
Art Director: Anahid Hamparian
Series designer: Symon Chow

Printed in China
1 3 5 6 4 2

CONTENTS

1 · THE PEOPLE OF THE COASTAL PLAIN

In the early 1600s English settlers established a colony on the coast of present-day Virginia. For the first few years they faced starvation. They were saved by Native American people from several tribes who had lived in the area for more than a hundred years. These people belonged to a confederacy, or union, of several tribes known as the Powhatan (Pow-uh-TAN). They brought corn, squash, wild turkeys, and fish to the hungry English, saving them from starvation.

The settlers thought they had landed in a barren wasteland because they did not know how to make use of the food the environment offered. The Powhatan knew how to hunt deer and turkey with bows and arrows, and how to catch small game, such as rabbits and squirrels, in snares. In the rivers, streams, and coastal waters, the Powhatan caught many

The village of Jamestown on the banks of the James River in about 1600

kinds of fish, and gathered clams, oysters, and other shellfish.

While the men hunted and fished, the women tended gardens, where they grew corn, several kinds of squash, beans, and sunflowers. In addition, the women and children gathered wild grapes and many varieties of berries, nuts, and edible roots, such as lilies and cattails.

The Powhatan lived in small villages in the coastal region of Virginia, a low-lying plain with many rivers and streams flowing from the Blue Ridge Mountains east into the Atlantic Ocean. This region is also called the Tidewater because the saltwater tide extends upstream for several miles. The waterways formed highways for the many tribes inhabiting the Atlantic coast. Paddling canoes hollowed out of single logs, they could travel swiftly and easily.

Although the climate in the Tidewater is comfortable in spring and fall, summers can be hot and steamy, with frequent thunderstorms. Winters are mild, but there is occasional snow, even on the coast. Snow is much more common

MARYLAND

VIRGINIA

Rappahannock River

Potomac River

Rappahannock

Pamunkey River

Mataponi River

Youghtanund

Pamunkey

Mattaponi

York River

CHESAPEAKE BAY

ATLANTIC OCEAN

James River

Chickahominy

Arrohateck

Appomatox River

Powhatan

JAMESTOWN

Chiskiack

Kecoughtan

James River

Appamatuck

Nansemond

This map of the Tidewater region shows the twelve tribes that made up the Powhatan Confederacy.

farther inland, however, where the land rises into the foothills of the Blue Ridge.

The people we call the Powhatan were actually made up of several tribes: the Pamunkey, Mattaponi, Chick-

Chief Powhatan on his throne

ahominy, and others. The scattered tribes had probably lived farther north on the coastal plain for a thousand years or more. Around 1600, six tribes were ruled by a powerful chief, named Wahunsonacock, but more commonly referred to by the title "Powhatan." Powhatan added other tribes to what is called the Powhatan Confederacy, named after Chief Powhatan. By the time the first English settlers came in 1607, he controlled about thirty tribes numbering about fourteen thousand people.

In 1607, 104 Englishmen and boys landed on a low-lying **peninsula**, where they started a colony they named Jamestown. This was the first English colony in North America and, for many years, the settlers struggled to survive. The swampy land was mosquito-infested, and many colonists died of malaria and other diseases. The Powhatan were friendly at first and gave the settlers gifts of food. As more ships brought more colonists, however, tensions increased and violent attacks by both sides became common.

In 1613 the colonists kidnapped Chief Powhatan's favorite daughter, Pocahontas. The young girl stayed at Jamestown, learned English, and married her teacher, John Rolfe. The marriage led to a few years of peace between the settlers and the Powhatan. Rolfe also gave Jamestown an economic boost by finding strains of West Indies tobacco that grew well in the Virginia soil. This crop brought huge profits, as

Tobacco gave the Jamestown settlers a vital cash crop.

well as more colonists and a demand for more and more Powhatan lands.

The sudden death of Pocahontas in England, followed by the death of her father the next year in 1618, led to a renewal of hostilities between the colonists and the Powhatan. Chief Powhatan was succeeded by his brother Opitchapam, but the real power was exercised by another brother named

Opechancanough. In 1622 Opechancanough gathered a strong force of warriors and launched the largest raid the English had yet faced. Out of about 1,200 colonists, 347 were massacred. The Powhatan chief assumed that such a brutal assault would cause the English to follow Indian practice and leave. Instead, the settlers fought back, burning Powhatan villages and crops, murdering women and children, and capturing some children to sell as slaves in the West Indies.

The attack of 1622 was followed by more than twenty years of warfare, with a few periods of uneasy peace. In 1644 Opechancanough, now in his eighties, decided to carry out one more great attack on the English. By this time, however, more than eight thousand colonists lived in Jamestown, whereas the Powhatan had been reduced to about five thousand people, mostly by diseases, like measles and smallpox, against which their bodies had no natural immunity.

The first assaults caused about five hundred English deaths, but the Powhatan had little hope of driving them out.

The Legend of Pocahontas

Powhatan was an intelligent and powerful chief who ruled over an estimated 130 villages at the time Jamestown was founded in 1607. He was friendly to the colonists at first, and he was aware that trade with the English could bring him useful things, such as tools and weapons made of iron.

When his men captured Captain John Smith, one of Jamestown's leaders, however, Powhatan showed his cruel side. He gave his warriors permission to smash in Smith's skull with rocks. Smith was saved when Powhatan's favorite daughter, Pocahontas, rushed forward, threw herself on Smith to protect him, and begged her father to release him. Powhatan relented and Smith's life was spared. Did this really happen? The legend has generally been accepted, although the only account we have of it was written by Smith himself several years later.

The rest of the Pocahontas story is known to be true. She was captured by the English and spent a year in Jamestown. She was extremely popular with the colonists, and her marriage to John Rolfe in 1614 assured several years of peace. Pocahontas traveled to England with Rolfe and was received there with great enthusiasm. The couple was preparing to return to Virginia in 1617 when Pocahontas became ill and died suddenly. Chief Powhatan was grief-stricken by the news of his daughter's death, and he died a few months later. The loss of Pocahontas and her father ended all hopes for a lasting peace between the Powhatan and the Jamestown settlers.

A nineteenth-century artist's version of Pocahontas saving the life of Captain John Smith

The colonists struck back quickly, but two years of bitter warfare were needed to crush the Powhatan resistance. Opechancanough was captured in 1646 and was taken to Jamestown, where the proud warrior refused to surrender or to sign a treaty. He was shot in the back and killed by an English guard who was acting without orders.

Chief Opechancanough rallied several tribes against the English.

Opechancanough's successor quickly signed treaties in 1646 and 1647 that restricted the Powhatan to several small areas, which later became **reservations**. None of these areas was large enough to sustain the tribe by their traditional life of hunting, gathering, and some farming. By 1722 the population of the Powhatan had declined to fewer than two thousand people. In a new treaty that year, many of the tribes that had made up the Powhatan Confederacy were reported to be extinct.

Over the next two hundred years, many of the Powhatan decided to find a place in mainstream American society. Some found work as servants and others as hunting guides. The reservations dwindled as settlers took more Powhatan lands. By the early 1800s only two tribes—the Pamunkey and the Accomac—still held land that was officially recognized as Indian.

Somehow, a few groups of Powhatan managed to cling to their identity through the nineteenth and twentieth centuries. Their original language was nearly lost, but other elements of their cultural traditions were not. In the late 1900s, like other native peoples throughout the United States and Canada, the Powhatan began to reorganize and look for ways to reclaim tribal lands.

2 · THE POWHATAN WAY OF LIFE

As dawn broke over the Atlantic Ocean, Powhatan villages sprang to life. Everyone had a task to do. Men were the hunters, fishermen, and warriors. With bows and stone-tipped arrows, they hunted deer and sometimes bear, as well as smaller game, such as rabbits, squirrels, wild turkeys, and geese. They used spears and nets to catch a variety of fish, and they also gathered oysters, clams, scallops, and other shellfish.

The men also made tools, weapons, and jewelry. Stone, wood, deer antlers, bones, and seashells provided the Powhatan with materials for tools, weapons, and houses. Shells were used to make scrapers for softening deer hide and other tasks. Quahog clam shells were used to make **wampum**, small beads that ranged in color from white to the

The Powhatan lived in harmony with their peaceful surroundings.

A Powhatan quiver made of reeds

more valuable purple. Many hours of labor were needed to make the beads, to drill holes through them, and to string them onto belts, bracelets, and other decorative items. Wampum belts were sometimes given to other tribes as a symbol of friendship or peace, but they were not used as money. The Powhatan tribes might trade goods, but they had no concept of money.

Powhatan men used tools made of stone and shells plus fire to build dugout canoes. They also helped make frames for houses by placing saplings in the ground, then bending the tops over to meet at the center, forming an arch or dome shape. The women did the rest of the construction work, and the houses belonged to them.

There were two kinds of houses in Powhatan villages. Smaller houses, called **wigwams,** were usually for one family. They were circular, with a domed roof. The larger houses, in which several families lived, were called **yehakins,** but the English colonists called them "longhouses." Both longhouses and wigwams were covered with sheets of bark or woven mats. A fire kept the houses warm in winter, and each

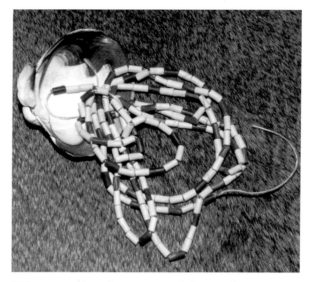

Wampum beads were used for trade.

Dug-out canoes provided swift transportation on the many streams.

Reconstructions of sturdy lodges show a Powhatan village as it may have looked in 1600.

family in a longhouse had its own fireplace for heat and for cooking. A small hole in the roof allowed some of the smoke to escape, but there were no windows, so the houses were usually smoky and dark. Larger villages had a council house and a storage building where smoked or dried foods were kept for use during winter. The village might also be surrounded by a stockade, or log wall.

A low bench ran around the inside of the houses. Parts of the bench, covered with furs or deerskins, were for sleeping. Other parts were used to store personal items, and bags of dried food were hung from racks close to the roof. In winter, when Powhatan families spent much of their time indoors, they sat on furs on the ground or on the bench. They played games, told stories, sang, and practiced music and dances for ceremonies.

According to accounts written by English colonists, Powhatan women worked very hard. They planted, tended, and harvested the crops of corn, squash, beans, and sunflowers. Children helped with the garden work. They were especially useful in small field shelters, from which they emerged to chase away birds and animal pests, such as rabbits, skunks, and woodchucks.

With the help of daughters over the age of eight or nine, women prepared the meals. Food was usually cooked in out-door fire pits. Meals were usually soups or thick stews made

Corn Soup

Native American tribes throughout eastern North America made this easy-to-prepare soup. In a thicker version it became corn stew. The clay pot was kept warm all day, and the Powhatan ate whenever they were hungry rather than at set mealtimes. You can make this recipe with fresh corn cut off the cob, or with canned corn. Corn soup is easy to make but you should always have an adult help you. You will need these ingredients:

- 2 to 3 ears of fresh corn, cut off the cob, or one 14-ounce can of whole kernel corn
- $1/2$ cup chopped clams, or cooked stewing beef in small chunks
- 6 to 8 leaves from fresh spinach, washed and uncooked

- about $1/2$ cup white or brown rice
- 1 quart water
- 1 teaspoon salt
- measuring cup and spoons
- 3- or 4-quart saucepan
- kitchen scissors
- wooden mixing spoon

Makes 3–4 servings

1. Drain the liquid off the can of corn. Put the corn in the saucepan and add the clams or cooked beef.
2. Cut the stems off the spinach and tear the leaves into small pieces. Add to the cooking pot.
3. Add the rice, water, and salt. Stir and bring to a boil over medium-high heat.
4. As soon as the mixture begins to boil, reduce the heat to simmer. Continue cooking until the rice is cooked—about 15 minutes for white rice and 25 to 30 minutes for brown rice. Serve hot.

Pieces of meat and corn are wrapped in corn leaves for roasting.

of beans, corn, squash, and sometimes bits of meat or fish, simmered in clay pots. Spits for roasting turkeys and other meats were made of sturdy green branches. The women parched, or toasted, bowls of corn in the ashes of the fire, then pounded it into a meal that was used to bake a flat bread.

Women also made all of the clothing. Men and older boys wore a breechcloth and, in colder weather, deerskin leggings. In winter they wore mantles, or cloaks, made of soft deerskin.

Powhatan Headband

Powhatan men wore simple headbands, rather than the elaborate headdresses common in the tribes of the Great Plains. Boys and girls also wore headbands, but they seem to have been used less frequently by adult women.

The headbands were decorated with dyed porcupine quills, small seashells, or beads. A feather or two completed the decoration. Feathers, beads, and sequins are available in craft or hobby stores, and in the craft section of discount department stores.

You will need:

- a few sheets of newspaper
- a strip of felt in any light color that measures 18 inches (46 cm) by 1 ¹/₂ inches (4 cm)
- a ruler
- a one-hole paper punch
- two rawhide laces (sold as shoelaces) or twine, each 10–12 inches (25–30 cm) long
- scissors
- white glue or craft glue
- red, blue, yellow, and black markers
- small sequins or beads in any colors (optional)
- one or two feathers

1· Spread the newspaper to protect your work surface.

2· Measure the felt strip so that it fits most of the way around your head, just above your eyes. Leave a gap of about 4 inches (10 cm) for tying the headband. Use the hole punch to make two holes about $1/4$ inch (.6 cm) from each end.

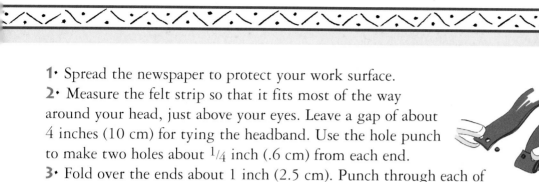

3· Fold over the ends about 1 inch (2.5 cm). Punch through each of the holes you made so that the punch goes through the second layer of fabric.

4· Unfold the ends and glue them back together with a thin layer of glue. Allow the glue to dry (about 10 minutes).

5· Run a piece of rawhide lace or twine through both holes in one end of the felt strip. About 2 inches (5 cm) beyond the edge of the strip, tie a double knot. Cut off one loose end of rawhide, but leave the other end long for tying the headband on your head.

6· Repeat step 5 with the other piece of lacing at the other end of the headband.

7· With the folds underneath, lay the headband flat. Use markers to make geometric or floral designs. Glue on sequins or beads if you wish.

8· Place a patch of felt over the quill end of the feather and glue the patch over the inside of the headband near the laces. The feather(s) can be straight up or tipped at an angle.

9· To wear the headband, tie the rawhide lace at the back of your head in a single knot and a bow (like tying a shoe).

The tribal leaders and their wives often wore mantles made of turkey feathers. The standard clothing for a woman was a knee-length skirt, topped by a shirt-like garment made of fringed deerskin or a cloak. Both men and women wore moccasins.

Men shaved the hair off the right side of their heads, so it would not get tangled with a bowstring or arrow during hunting or warfare. Married women kept their hair long, usually worn in a single braid down the back. Young girls had the front

A deer hide is stretched on a frame for curing and drying.

and sides of their head shaved close, with the rest of their hair worn down the back in a braid. Women often were tattooed on their bodies, arms, and faces. Men were less likely to have tattoos, but they did paint their faces and bodies before games, ceremonies, or war.

Although the Powhatan lived in settled villages, the entire community moved every few years. The moves were made when the soil became worn out from growing the same crops year after year. New farmland was cleared by cutting and burning shrubs and undergrowth. The ash from these fires provided good fertilizer for the first planting.

The abandoned land continued to be controlled by the tribe, and any group within the tribe could move onto the land or use it. No one actually owned land; the Powhatan did not understand the European concept of land ownership. This became one cause of conflict between colonists, who claimed to own the land, and the Indians, who thought the land was there for everyone to use.

3 · CUSTOMS AND BELIEFS

Like nearly all Native American cultures, the Powhatan believed in a variety of gods, all of them related to objects or forces in nature, such as the sun, moon, thunder, and wind. Every living thing had a soul or spirit that the people did not want to offend. They developed many rituals to protect themselves from spirits that could harm them.

A hunter asked for forgiveness from the soul of any animal he killed, hoping that the animal spirit would not seek revenge. The bones of the animal were treated with respect and returned to the forest. The bones of fish were returned to the water. When a hunter was successful, he had to make sure that all the meat from the animal killed was used. He could give it away to others in the village or he might have a huge feast, even inviting another village. It was

Carved poles form a circle for ceremonial dances.

Powhatan Seasons

Because the Powhatan lived so close to nature, their customs, beliefs, and ceremonies were all related to the natural world. Even their names for the seasons reflected this closeness to nature and led them to identify five seasons, rather than four:

1• "The blossoming of spring": This season would probably be March and April, plus parts of late February and early May.

2• "The first earing of corn," or "the time of roasting the young ears": This season spans May, June, and early July.

3• "The summer sun": This season occurs when the sun is hottest, through early September.

4• "The corn harvest" or "the falling of the leaf": This season corresponds to fall, and stretches into December.

5• "cohonk," or winter: *Cohonk* is the Powhatan word for the sound made by the migrating geese that arrive in December through early February.

important to avoid angering the animal's spirit by wasting anything.

The Powhatan had a major god named **Okeus**, who was associated with the burial of the dead. They made images of Okeus and placed them with the deceased. Burials differed according to the importance of the person. For common people the body was wrapped in skins, placed in a deep hole, and covered with soil. The bones of chiefs, important healers, and great warriors were wrapped in mats and placed in a burial house.

In their efforts to live well and avoid things that could harm them, such as lightning or floods, the Powhatan placed great emphasis on dreams. A person, usually a man, who could use dreams to find the cause and the cure of an illness became a **shaman**, or healer. Most families relied on the village shaman when there was illness. Shamans used special rituals, potions, and dreams to find a cure.

The Powhatan also placed a lot of confidence in the dreams of family members. Mothers asked their children

A Powhatan Creation Story

The Powhatan have many stories about how human life began. This is one of the most popular.

In the beginning the great Earth Mother had two sons named Glooskap and Malsum. Glooskap was good and wise. When the Earth Mother died, he began to create plants, animals, and humans. His brother, Malsum, however, was selfish and evil. He made poisonous plants and snakes, and began plotting to kill Glooskap.

Malsum pestered Glooskap with questions, trying to find his weakness. Glooskap could not tell a lie, so he finally confessed that the only thing that could kill him was an owl feather. Malsum sneaked off and made a dart from an owl feather, then used it to kill his brother.

The evil Malsum, however, did not realize that because Glooskap was all good, he could not be killed. Glooskap also knew that he could not allow Malsum to stay in the world and so, reluctantly, Glooskap killed his evil brother. Glooskap, now free from his brother, completed his task of making all the plants, animals, and humans. Malsum's spirit went deep into the earth, where he became a wicked wolf-spirit. To this day he sometimes torments humans and animals.

Accompanied by his sacred rattle, a shaman uses his skills to cure a patient.

to describe their dreams each morning. The Powhatan believed that a dream could foretell future events or reveal some skill or talent that should be encouraged.

When a boy reached age thirteen, he might go on a **vision quest**. This involved living apart from the village for several days, eating little, and sitting very still to try to induce a trance or dream. If it worked, the boy would report his vision to the elders of the village. They would then decide if the boy should become a shaman.

Sometimes a dream might suggest that a youth should be prepared to become a *weroance* (chief) or a warrior. The major chief of a tribe inherited the position through the female side of the family. Every village also chose a lesser chief. A boy chosen to be groomed for leadership went through a grueling nine-month ordeal of fasting, visions, and physical hardship.

The Powhatan not only relied on dreams, but they also had a remarkable knowledge of herbal medicine. In the eighteenth and nineteenth centuries, settlers learned a great deal about natural cures from the Powhatan and other tribes.

Important occasions in the life of the tribe, such as preparing for war or celebrating a victory or a great harvest, were observed with special songs and dances. The main instruments were rattles and drums.

Rattles were made of dried gourds or turtle shells, with seeds or pebbles inside for sound. The Powhatan made several kinds of drums. The most popular was a water drum, made of deerskin stretched over a hollowed-out log. Enough water

A Powhatan drum

was added to create the desired tone. The result was a booming beat to accompany the dancers.

4 · THE PRESENT AND THE FUTURE

The Powhatan nearly vanished in the years after their defeat in 1644 and having their land restricted to reservations. Since these reservations were too small to support the Powhatan's traditional way of life, many Powhatan went to work for colonists on Virginia plantations (large farms that specialized in a single crop, such as tobacco).

By the 1890s the Powhatan were limited to a few hundred people living on the Pamunkey and Mattaponi reservations. These were two of the original reservations established in 1644, making them the oldest Indian reservations in the country.

Over the years, the Pamunkey managed to hold onto some of their original lands near the town of West Point, even after those lands were divided in the 1700s. Some of the people

Natural beauty on the Pamunkey Indian Reservation

living on the banks of the Mattaponi River formed a separate Powhatan tribe called the Mattaponi and received official recognition from the government of Virginia.

Encouraged by the example of the Mattaponi, other groups of related families began to reorganize their tribes. They drew others from the northern states and Canada. The Chickahominy tribe was reorganized in the early 1900s, and the Eastern Chickahominy in 1925. Three other Powhatan tribes—Nansemond, Rappahonnock, and Upper Mattaponi —were also organized after 1920, but they did not live on reservations, so they had no land and no official status.

In the 1960s and 1970s the members of the various Powhatan tribes worked hard to rediscover and preserve their traditional way of life. The Pamunkey, for example, who had long been known for their pottery, began to use modern marketing techniques to generate income from their craft. Other skills were taught to younger generations, and festivals were held to bring members of different tribes together to share ways of preserving crafts, songs and dances, and Powhatan stories.

By the 1980s state and federal governments were responding to the needs of Native Americans. In 1983 the Virginia General Assembly established the Virginia Council on Indians, made up of nine tribal representatives. The mission of the council is to promote programs in education, health care, and social matters for the state's Indians. The General Assembly also gave official recognition to the six tribes organized in the 1900s. Two more tribes were granted official status in 1990.

A young member of the Chickahominy tribe dances in traditional clothing.

There are now an estimated three thousand Powhatan scattered through the coastal areas of Virginia.

The Powhatan have become increasingly involved in activities to revive, or bring back, their traditional beliefs and customs. Like other Native American societies, they now organize celebrations called **powwows**. The public is often invited to these events where they can sample Powhatan crafts, traditional music and dance, and foods.

A number of Powhatan have become involved in reviving their original **Algonquian** language. The language, as it developed in Virginia, had not been spoken for the past two hundred years. By relying on the Algonquian language used throughout Canada and on the Atlantic coast, a modern version of the language is now being taught to young Powhatan students.

Powhatan Words and Phrases

Since the Powhatan version of the Algonquian language has not been used since 1800, the words and phrases the people speak today are based on other versions of Algonquian and by early sources, including Thomas Jefferson, who wrote one of the few accounts of the Powhatan language. The following words come from an even earlier book, the *Dictionary of Powhatan*, which was compiled in the 1600s.

Words

English	Powhatan	English	Powhatan
one	*Nekut*	man	*Nimatew*
two	*Ninge*	woman	*Crenepo*
three	*Nus*	dog	*Attemous*
four	*Yough*	sun	*Keshowse*
five	*Paranske*	moon	*Umpsquoth*

Phrases

Good luck attend you.	*Aupadush shawaindaugozzeyun.*
What is your name?	*Auneen dizheekauzoyun?*
Where do you live?	*Auneende aindauyun?*
What do you want?	*Waigonain wau iayun?*

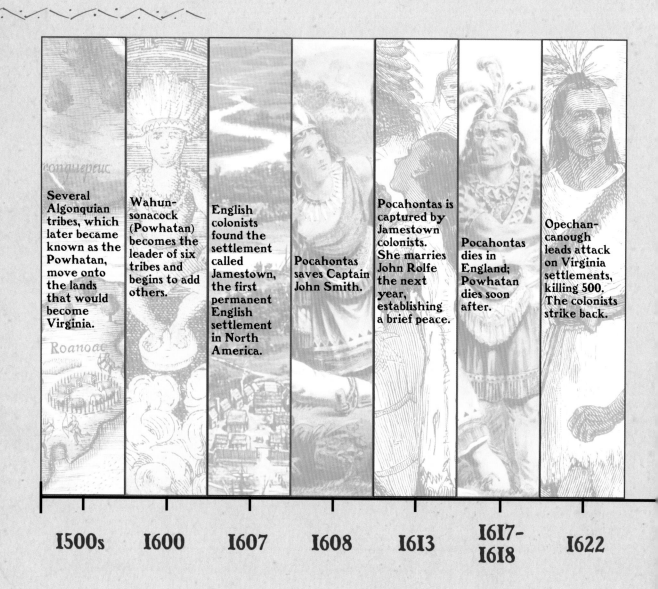

Several Algonquian tribes, which later became known as the Powhatan, move onto the lands that would become Virginia.

Wahun-sonacock (Powhatan) becomes the leader of six tribes and begins to add others.

English colonists found the settlement called Jamestown, the first permanent English settlement in North America.

Pocahontas saves Captain John Smith.

Pocahontas is captured by Jamestown colonists. She marries John Rolfe the next year, establishing a brief peace.

Pocahontas dies in England; Powhatan dies soon after.

Opechancanough leads attack on Virginia settlements, killing 500. The colonists strike back.

1500s 1600 1607 1608 1613 1617–1618 1622

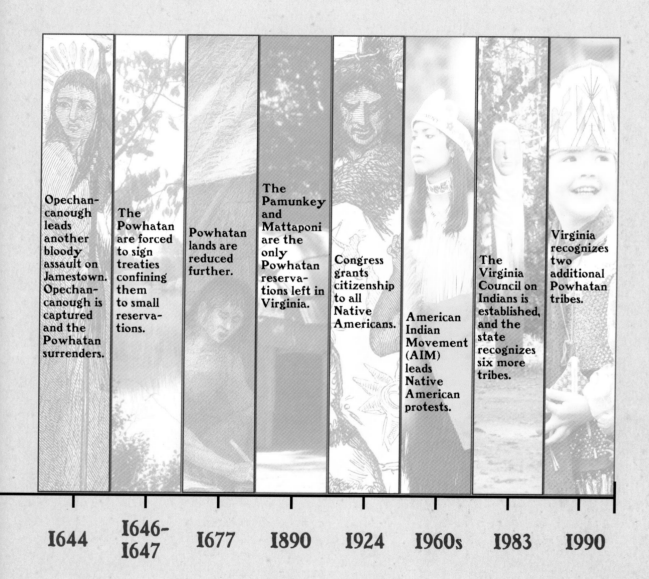

Opechan-canough leads another bloody assault on Jamestown. Opechan-canough is captured and the Powhatan surrenders.

The Powhatan are forced to sign treaties confining them to small reservations.

Powhatan lands are reduced further.

The Pamunkey and Mattaponi are the only Powhatan reservations left in Virginia.

Congress grants citizenship to all Native Americans.

American Indian Movement (AIM) leads Native American protests.

The Virginia Council on Indians is established, and the state recognizes six more tribes.

Virginia recognizes two additional Powhatan tribes.

1644

1646-1647

1677

1890

1924

1960s

1983

1990

· GLOSSARY

Algonquian: A group of Algonquian-speaking tribes living on the Atlantic Coast, as well as New England, southern Canada, and the Great Lakes.

cohonk: The Powhatan word for "winter"; the word is meant to sound like the "honk" of migrating geese.

Okeus: The major god of the Powhatan.

peninsula: A piece of land surrounded by water on three sides.

powwow: A Native American celebration at which others are invited to sample Indian crafts, music and dance, and foods.

reservation: Land set aside by a government as a home for Native Americans.

shaman: A spiritual leader and healer.

vision quest: A youth's search for a special vision or dream.

wampum: Beads strung on a belt and used by many Native American nations as a means of exchange.

wigwams: Circular Powhatan dwellings, usually for one family, made of saplings bent to form a dome and covered with bark.

yehakins: Long dwellings with curved roofs made of sapling frames covered with bark.

· FIND OUT MORE

Books

Bruchal, Joseph. *Pocahontas*. New York: Harcourt, 2005.

Ford, Carin. *Pocahontas: American Indian Princess*. Berkeley Heights, NJ: Enslow Publishers, 2006.

Kalman, Bobbie, and Rebecca Sjonger. *Life of the Powhatan*. New York: Crabtree Publishing Co., 2004.

Sita, Lisa. *Pocahontas: The Powhatan Culture and the Jamestown Colony*. New York: PowerKids Press, 2005.

Williams, Suzanne. *Powhatan Indians*. Chicago: Heinemann/ Raintree, 2003.

org

ginia

mseyil/vaindianspowindex.htm

rd-winning author who has written
ks for children and young adults,
e *Nez Perce*, and *The Sioux* in the First
nd his wife, Sharon, live in the
n of New York, Massachusetts, and
ls have taken them through most of

• INDEX

Page numbers in **boldface** are illustrations.